Romeo and Juliet
Classroom Questions

A SCENE BY SCENE TEACHING GUIDE

Amy Farrell

SCENE BY SCENE
ENNISKERRY, IRELAND

Copyright © 2015 by Amy Farrell.

All rights reserved. No part of this publication may be reproduced, distributed or transmitted in any form or by any means, including photocopying, recording, or other electronic or mechanical methods, without the prior written permission of the publisher, except in the case of brief quotations embodied in critical reviews and certain other noncommercial uses permitted by copyright law.

Scene by Scene
11 Millfield, Enniskerry
Wicklow, Ireland.
www.scenebysceneguides.com

Romeo and Juliet Classroom Questions by Amy Farrell. —1st ed.
ISBN 978-1-910949-31-3

Contents

Prologue	1
Act One, Scene One	3
Act One, Scene Two	6
Act One, Scene Three	8
Act One, Scene Four	10
Act One, Scene Five	12
Act Two, Scene One	14
Act Two, Scene Two	16
Act Two, Scene Three	18
Act Two, Scene Four	20
Act Two, Scene Five	22
Act Two, Scene Six	24
Act Three, Scene One	26
Act Three, Scene Two	30
Act Three, Scene Three	32
Act Three, Scene Four	34
Act Three, Scene Five	36
Act Four, Scene One	39
Act Four, Scene Two	41
Act Four, Scene Three	43
Act Four, Scene Four	45
Act Four, Scene Five	47

Act Five, Scene One	49
Act Five, Scene Two	51
Act Five, Scene Three	53
General Questions	55

Prologue

Points to Consider

The prologue gives a brief overview of the action of the play. As such, analysing its content prepares students for the plot of the story, pre-teaching the tale to come.

Discussing the prologue is a good way to discover what students know about the play, and what their expectations may be.

Prologues of this nature rarely occur in modern film or drama. It can be interesting to discuss why this is the case.

Questions

1. What information about the play do we receive in the prologue?

2. What do you already know about *Romeo and Juliet*?

Act One, Scene One

Points to Consider

This scene introduces the houses of Montague and Capulet and the feud between their families.

Conflict and violence are established as major themes.

Romeo is in love when we meet him, something that often catches students off guard. Their expectations and surprise at this are worth discussing, as is the topic of the nature of love.

Questions

1. As the scene begins, what are Gregory and Sampson planning to do?

2. In line 18 Gregory says "This quarrel is between our masters, and us their men." What does this mean?

3. Gregory boasts about starting fights and overpowering women. What does this tell you about the men?

4. Sampson says he will bite his thumb at the Montague men. In your opinion, what could be the modern day equivalent of this gesture?

5. When Benvolio arrives he shouts, "Part, fools! Put up your swords." What does this tell you about his attitude to violence?

6. Tybalt says, "What, drawn and talk of peace? I hate the word as I hate hell, all Montagues, and thee."
What does this tell you about his character?

7. What does the Prince threaten will happen if there is more violence on the streets of Verona?

8. How does Montague describe the behaviour of his son, Romeo?

9. Why is Romeo so unhappy?

10. Romeo says, "This is not Romeo, he's some other where". What has affected his personality so much?

11. Benvolio advises Romeo to "Examine other beauties". What do you think of this advice?

Act One, Scene Two

Points to Consider

Juliet's arranged marriage and the character of her father are interesting points raised by this scene.

Students are introduced to Paris, another important character.

Questions

1. As the scene begins, does Capulet think Juliet is ready to marry Paris?

2. Do you think Paris is eager to marry Juliet? Explain.

3. What do Romeo and Benvolio find out from Capulet's servant?

4. Benvolio tells Romeo to,
   "Compare her face with some that I shall show,
   And I will make thee think thy swan a crow".
   What does this mean?

Act One, Scene Three

Points to Consider

Juliet's relationship with her mother, Lady Capulet, and the Nurse are worth considering here.

The topic of arranged marriage can be further considered in light of Juliet's response to her parents' plans for her future.

Questions

1. What are your first impressions of the Nurse?

2. When asked about marriage, Juliet says, "It is an honour that I dream not of." What does this tell you about her?

3. Is Juliet's mother keen for her to marry Paris? Explain.

4. What does the Nurse think of Paris?

5. What does Juliet agree to do?

Act One, Scene Four

Points to Consider

Romeo is presented as a serious, downcast youth in this scene. It is interesting to discuss his behaviour, considering he is on his way to a grand feast.

The question of whether or not Romeo is actually in love with Rosaline should be considered. If he is not in love, why does he behave as he does?

Attention should be drawn to Romeo's prophetic dream, as destiny is a theme to be considered.

Mercutio's character is developed in this scene.

Questions

1. Why does Romeo "have a soul of lead"?

2. Romeo says, "Under love's heavy burden do I sink". Does he sound like somebody who is really in love?

3. In what ways is Mercutio different to Romeo?

4. Romeo says,
   "my mind misgives
   some consequence, yet hanging in the stars,
   shall bitterly begin his fearful date with this
   night's revels."
   What does this mean?
   What is your response to this?

Act One, Scene Five

Points to Consider

Romeo is mesmerised from the moment he first lays eyes on Juliet. This can lead to an interesting discussion on the existence of love at first sight.

Tybalt's outrage when he sees Romeo develops the concept of the feud between the families and is worth noting. It also shows him to be a short-tempered, hot-headed character.

The idea of the "star-crossed" or ill-fated lovers is set up once Juliet realises who Romeo is, having fallen in love with him immediately at the feast. These ideas of true love, love at first sight, and destiny, can make for lively classroom discussion.

Questions

1. What kind of host is Capulet?

2. What is Romeo's immediate reaction when he sees Juliet?

3. Romeo says,
   "Did my heart love till now? Forswear it, sight!
   For I ne'er saw true beauty till this night."
   What does this mean?

4. What is Tybalt's reaction when he recognises Romeo at the feast?

5. How does Capulet react to Romeo's presence?

6. How does Juliet react to Romeo?

7. When Romeo realises Juliet is a Capulet he says, "My life is my foe's debt". What does this mean?

8. Juliet says to the Nurse,
   "Go ask his name – If he be married,
   My grave is like to be my wedding bed".
   What does this tell us?

9. Do you think the feud between the families will make Juliet try to keep away from Romeo? Explain.

Act Two, Scene One

Points to Consider

Students sometimes wonder why Romeo gives his friends the slip here, and it can add to their understanding of his developing character if this is discussed in class.

Mercutio assumes that Romeo is still in love with Rosaline in this scene. This comment can lead to an interesting discussion of the fickle nature of love and whether Romeo can in fact truly love Juliet already.

Questions

1. Why can't Benvolio and Mercutio find Romeo?

2. Do you think Mercutio takes love seriously? Explain.

Act Two, Scene Two

Points to Consider

This is the famous 'Balcony Scene' that many students will already know something of. Discussing their current knowledge of it and experiences of references to it in literature, film, etc. can build anticipation and excitement around this scene.

Students may enjoy recognising famous quotations in this scene.

It is interesting to re-visit the 'true love' debate after studying this scene. Often, sceptical students are won over by the emotional language and declarations of love.

Romeo has been transformed due to his love for Juliet. The moody petulance of earlier scenes is no more.

Questions

1. Romeo says that Mercutio, "jests at scars that never felt a wound". How is Mercutio different to Romeo?

2. How do you know that Romeo thinks Juliet is beautiful?

3. Juliet says,
   "wherefore art thou Romeo?
   Deny thy father and refuse thy name.
   Or, if thou wilt not, be but sworn my love,
   And I'll no longer be a Capulet".
   What does this mean and why does she say it?

4. Why doesn't Romeo reveal himself to Juliet straight away?

5. How would you feel if you were overheard as Juliet is here?

6. Why does Romeo disregard the danger of being caught in the orchard?

7. What kind of person is Juliet? Explain.

8. What view of love do the couple have? Explain.

Act Two, Scene Three

Points to Consider

Students sometimes find it difficult to understand what Friar Laurence is doing as this scene begins. It can be useful to explain the practice of making herbal remedies, etc. His skills here will be called on later on, so it is important to flag them for students at this point.

Romeo has changed entirely from the moody teenager we met in the opening moments of the play. Students will enjoy discussing the nature of this transformation, and whether it proves that Romeo is really in love.

In this scene, Romeo announces his intention to marry Juliet to the Friar. Students will enjoy discussing whether this is a hasty match, and what Friar Laurence's motivations could be for helping Romeo.

Questions

1. What is Friar Laurence doing as the scene begins?

2. Romeo tells Friar Laurence,
"With Rosaline, my ghostly father? No.
I have forgot that name and that name's woe."
What do you think of the way he has forgotten Rosaline so quickly?

3. "Then plainly know my heart's dear love is set,
On the fair daughter of rich Capulet.
As mine on hers, so hers is set on mine."
Do you think Romeo and Juliet are rushing into this marriage?

4. Friar Laurence tells Romeo,
"O, she knew well,
Thy love did read by rote and could not spell"
when he speaks of Romeo's love for Rosaline. How has Romeo's attitude to, and understanding of, love changed?

5. Why does Friar Laurence help Romeo?

Act Two, Scene Four

Points to Consider

Tybalt's challenge escalates the issue of the feud between the families.

Mercutio's view of love is worth discussing and contrasting with that of Romeo.

In this scene the Nurse's devotion to Juliet is evident. It is worth considering as it can be compared to the way that Juliet's parents treat her later on.

Questions

1. What is Mercutio's attitude to love?

2. How has Romeo's mood changed since his last conversation with his friends? Explain.

3. Before the Nurse delivers Juliet's message to Romeo, what does she warn him of?

4. What is Romeo's message for Juliet?

Act Two, Scene Five

Points to Consider

Students enjoy discussing how they would react if they had to wait for important news as Juliet does in this scene.

Questions

1. Why is Juliet impatient with the Nurse's absence?

2. "Do you not see that I am out of breath?"
   Why does the Nurse delay in telling Juliet her news?

3. What kind of person is the Nurse, based on what you have seen of her so far?

Act Two, Scene Six

Points to Consider

It is worth discussing the Friar's advice to 'love moderately' in this scene.

Romeo and Juliet cement their vows of love from the Balcony Scene in this scene. Mature insights can arise from a discussion of this secret marriage and its merits and flaws.

Questions

1. Friar Laurence advises Romeo to "love moderately". Explain what this means and why he might give this advice.

2. Do you think Romeo and Juliet truly love each other? Explain.

Act Three, Scene One

Points to Consider

Consider how tension is built in this scene, beginning with Benvolio's unease and foreboding.

This is an excellent scene to consider as 'a scene involving conflict'.

This is the turning point of the tragedy, where everything begins to fall asunder for the young couple.

Sometimes students feel that Romeo doesn't stand up for himself when Tybalt insults him and calls him 'villain'. Other students will argue that it shows not cowardice, but his love for Juliet. These opposing views can lead to lively classroom discussion.

Sometimes students feel that Romeo is responsible for Mercutio's wounding and death in a very literal sense, as he was, "hurt under your (Romeo's) arm". This can also be worth discussing.

It can be interesting to discuss whether Romeo's rage and desire for vengeance is justified, or whether these are the hot-headed actions of a boy.

This conflict further escalates the family feud separating the young couple.

It can be worthwhile to consider whether this conflict and unfortunate turn of events was in fact fated for Romeo and Juliet. Some students will feel that this was bound to happen sooner or later, others will argue that the marriage, once made public, could have resolved the family feud.

Questions

1. Benvolio warns Mercutio that,
   "The day is hot, the Capels abroad.
   And if we meet we shall not 'scape a brawl,
   For now, these hot days, is the mad blood stirring."
   How has the mood changed from the previous scene?

2. Mercutio says "Make it a word and a blow" to Tybalt.
   What is he doing here?

3. How does Tybalt treat Benvolio, Mercutio and Romeo in this scene?

4. Why does Romeo try to avoid fighting with Tybalt?

5. Romeo tells Tybalt,
   "And so, good Capulet, which name I tender
   As dearly as my own, be satisfied".
   Why does this annoy Mercutio?

6. Mercutio tells Romeo, "Ask for me tomorrow, and you shall find me a grave man".
   What does this tell you about his injury?

7. What changes Romeo's mind and makes him want to fight with Tybalt?

8. When Lady Capulet sees Tybalt fallen she tells the Prince,
   "Prince, as thou art true,
   For blood of ours shed blood of Montague".
   What does this tell you about her character?

9. Lady Capulet says of Benvolio, "Affection makes him false. He speaks not true."
   Is this a fair accusation to make of Benvolio?

10. What punishment does the Prince decide on?

11. What curse does Mercutio wish on the Montagues and Capulets in this scene?

12. Comment on the atmosphere at this point in the play.

Act Three, Scene Two

Points to Consider

Students often feel sorry for Juliet as she eagerly awaits her husband, as she doesn't realise what has just occurred on the streets of Verona.

Juliet's reaction to the Nurse's initial garbled message and the real news are worth discussing.

It is interesting to discuss Juliet's maturity and strength of character in this scene.

Questions

1. As the scene begins, why is Juliet looking forward to the night?

2. Why is the Nurse so upset when she arrives?

3. Do you think Juliet forgives Romeo for killing Tybalt too quickly? Explain.

4. What is Juliet's reaction when she hears Romeo has been banished?

5. The Nurse tells Juliet,
   "I'll find Romeo
   To comfort you",
   even though she is upset herself over Tybalt's death. What does this tell you about the Nurse's character?

Act Three, Scene Three

Points to Consider

Students often enjoy discussing Romeo's reaction to his banishment.

It can be worthwhile to list and discuss the various obstacles in the path of the young lovers at this point. Similarly, it can be interesting to speculate about possible outcomes.

Questions

1. What is Romeo's reaction to being banished?

2. How does Friar Laurence view Romeo's banishment?

3. How does the Nurse react to Romeo's tears?

4. Friar Laurence tells Romeo, "Thy tears are womanish". What do you think of Romeo's tears and upset?

5. What reasons does Friar Laurence give Romeo to be happy?

6. What plan does Friar Laurence have for Romeo?

Act Three, Scene Four

Points to Consider

It can be interesting to discuss Capulet's plan to marry Juliet to Paris, considering her young age and her cousin's recent untimely death. Students often have strong views on this issue, that are worth exploring.

Questions

1. Does Juliet have any say in her proposed marriage to Paris?

2. What is your opinion of this arranged marriage?

3. How do you think Juliet will react to news of this marriage?

Act Three, Scene Five

Points to Consider

This is the last time we will see Romeo and Juliet happily together, so it is worth analysing their relationship at this point, and considering whether this is in fact 'true love'. Also, this will be a reference point for students when considering later scenes.

Students are often outraged by the way Juliet is treated by her parents. This can lead to lively discussions of the generation gap, and also of parent-child expectations and relationships.

The Nurse, who has been Juliet's steadfast friend and supporter up to this point, lets her down when she suggests that Juliet should go ahead and marry Paris. This can be interesting to discuss, as can the theme of friendship itself.

Students tend to engage well with considering matters from Juliet's point of view and empathising in this scene. It can be rewarding to work with students' personal and emotional responses to the action here.

Questions

1. Why does Juliet claim "it was the nightingale" they heard outside?

2. What makes her change her mind and tell Romeo, "O, now be gone!"?

3. Describe Romeo and Juliet's relationship at this point.

4. Why does Juliet ask Romeo, "O, thinkest thou we shall ever meet again?"
   How does this question of Juliet's make you feel?

5. Do you think the young couple are particularly unlucky? Explain.

6. Lady Capulet tells Juliet,
   "Some grief shows much of love;
   But much of grief shows still some want of wit".
   What does this tell you about her character?

7. What reason does Juliet give for refusing to marry Paris?

8. Lady Capulet remarks, "I would the fool were married to her grave!" when Juliet disobeys her.
   Comment on this statement.

9. How does Capulet react to Juliet's disobedience?

10. What is your opinion of how Juliet's parents are treating her, considering her cousin was killed on the previous day?

11. What is the Nurse's advice for Juliet?

12. What do you think of this advice?

13. Do you feel sorry for Juliet in this scene? Explain.

Act Four, Scene One

Points to Consider

Students often dislike Paris, they see him as an obstacle to Romeo and Juliet's happiness, so they often judge him unfairly. Bearing that in mind, it is interesting to discuss his behaviour towards Juliet, his intended bride, in this scene.

It is worth discussing whether the actions of both Friar Laurence and Juliet are too hasty in this scene.

Juliet's actions and desperate resolve are interesting to discuss in relation to the theme of 'true love'.

Questions

1. Why has Juliet come to Friar Laurence?

2. What is Juliet prepared to do, rather than marry Paris?

3. What plan does Friar Laurence devise for her?

4. Do you expect this behaviour from a holy man? Explain.

5. Do you think Juliet is brave to agree to a plan like this?

Act Four, Scene Two

Points to Consider

Juliet is completely isolated and alone as she follows the Friar's plan here.

Her parents are quick to accept that she has changed her mind, they care little about the reasons behind it.

Questions

1. Juliet tells her parents, "Henceforward I am ever ruled by you." Why are they so quick to believe her?

2. Do you think Capulet is excited at the prospect of his daughter's marriage? Explain.

3. Is it fair to describe Juliet as very isolated at this point? Explain your view.

Act Four, Scene Three

Points to Consider

It is worth considering Juliet's relationships with her mother and her Nurse, and how they differ.

This is make or break time for Juliet. Some students may feel she goes through with the plan as she is trapped, with no alternative, while others will argue that her actions are determined by her love for Romeo. Considering her motivation can make for lively classroom discussion.

It is interesting to discuss Juliet's character and whether or not she is truly brave.

Questions

1. Is Juliet closer to the Nurse or her mother? Explain your answer.

2. What worries and doubts does Juliet have about following the Friar's plan?

3. How would you feel, in her position?

Act Four, Scene Four

Points to Consider

This scene provides momentary relief and a change of pace from the preceding tension. Some students will find discussion of it frustrating, as they want to find out what happens next.

Questions

1. This scene is uneventful. What purpose does it serve?

Act Four, Scene Five

Points to Consider

It is interesting to discuss the various characters' reactions to the discovery of Juliet's 'body' in this scene.

Some students will have little sympathy for the Capulets here, feeling that they caused the sorrow they're feeling themselves.

Questions

1. How does the Nurse react when she discovers Juliet?

2. How does Lady Capulet react?

3. How has Capulet's attitude to Juliet changed?

4. Do you feel sorry for Juliet's parents here?

Act Five, Scene One

Points to Consider

Consider how Romeo's dream adds to the atmosphere here and lends itself to the theme of destiny ("I dreamt my lady came and found me dead").

Romeo's reaction to the news of Juliet's death is noteworthy. He is decisive and acts immediately, without giving way to emotion. Students usually enjoy discussing the change in his character since the beginning of the play and possible reasons for it.

It can be interesting to discuss the apothecary's actions here. Some will excuse his sale of the poison to Romeo, others will condemn him for it.

Questions

1. What dream has Romeo had?

2. What news does Balthasar bring Romeo?

3. How does Romeo react to the news of Juliet's 'death'?

4. What changes do you notice in Romeo?

5. What does Romeo plan to do?

6. What makes the apothecary sell Romeo the poison?

Act Five, Scene Two

Points to Consider

Some students may not realise what an "infectious pestilence" or plague involved, so it may be necessary to explain 'quarantine', in order for them to fully understand what has happened.

Friar Laurence is full of concern for Juliet, fearing that she is about to awaken alone in her crypt. It can be interesting to let students discuss how they would react in such circumstances.

Questions

1. What reason does John give for failing to deliver Friar Laurence's letter to Romeo?

2. Is this a frustrating turn of events?

3. What does Friar Laurence plan to do next?

4. What makes this a tense moment in the play?

Act Five, Scene Three

Points to Consider

Even though your students know the outcome of the play, they may still find it disappointing; many find it frustrating to see love thwarted so cruelly in the end. Bear this in mind, as often capable students are annoyed by the ending, and their initial answers may seem sub-par.

Paris' appearance at the graveyard raises some interesting ideas. Some students will pity him and feel he truly felt for Juliet, while others will have little sympathy, feeling he never really knew her enough to care about her. These polar views can make for lively discussion.

Similarly, Romeo's treatment of Paris will raise a number of responses. Some students will defend Romeo's actions, while others will feel his slaying of Paris is unnecessary and even cruel.

Generally, students will have views on the tomb scene and the actions of the young lovers. These will range from agreeing with their actions, given their circumstances, to dismissing them as immature. It is worthwhile to give some time over to allow students to express these views.

Questions

1. Why has Paris visited the graveyard?

2. Do you think Paris really loved Juliet? Explain.

3. What reason does Romeo give Balthasar for being in the tomb?

4. Why has Romeo come to the tomb, according to Paris?

5. Why does Romeo ask Paris to "O, be gone!"?

6. Do you feel sorry for Paris in this scene?

7. Why does Romeo place Paris in the tomb?

8. Do Romeo's actions here reveal anything about his personality?

9. When Friar Laurence realises his plan has gone terribly wrong, what alternative does he offer Juliet?

10. Are Romeo and Juliet responsible for taking their own lives? Explain.

11. What has happened to Lady Montague?

12. Do you think peace in Verona comes at too high a price?

13. Is this a moving scene? Explain your view.

General Questions

1. How do Romeo and Juliet mature during the play?

2. What different types of love are evident in the play?

3. What makes this play sad and tragic?

4. Is there any character that you particularly liked or disliked? Explain your answer.

5. Do you think that it was Romeo and Juliet's destiny to die in this way? What makes you say this? What hints were there in the play to suggest this outcome?

6. What does the play tell us about the way parents and the older generation try to control their children?

CLASSROOM QUESTIONS GUIDES

Short books of questions, designed to save teachers time and lead to rewarding classroom experiences.

www.SceneBySceneGuides.com
www.facebook.com/scenebyscene

www.ingramcontent.com/pod-product-compliance
Lightning Source LLC
Chambersburg PA
CBHW071321080526
44587CB00018B/3310